The Marble Orchard

Sandeep Parmar

The Marble Orchard

Shearsman Books

First published in the United Kingdom in 2012 by
Shearsman Books
50 Westons Hill Drive
Emersons Green
Bristol
BS16 7DF

Shearsman Books Ltd Registered Office
30–31 St. James Place, Mangotsfield, Bristol BS16 9JB
(this address not for correspondence)

www.shearsman.com

ISBN 978-1-84861-204-4

Acknowledgements
The author is grateful to the editors of the following magazines and
anthologies in which some of these poems first appeared:

*Best American Poetry Blog, The Black Herald, Cimarron Review, Contains
Small Parts: UEA Creative Writing Anthology, Eyewear, The Forward Book of
Poetry 2008, The HarperCollins Book of Modern English Poetry by Indians, The
Literary Review, Lung Jazz: Oxfam Book of Emerging British Poets, Magma,
The Manhattan Review, nthposition, Poetry International, Stand, Voice
Recognition: 21 Poets for the 21st Century* (Bloodaxe Books),
Washington Square Review, The Wolf and
World Literature Today.

Contents

I

Invocation	11
The Octagonal Tower	12
Archive for a Daughter	15
Recuerdelo	19
Against Chaos	20
June 16, 1956. The Church of St. George the Martyr	22
Newnham Portraits	24
Chopin's Waltz No. 7	26
Loy Returns to Paris	27
Tartarus	28
Ambracia	29
Ephyre	30
The White Sister	31
Beatified	32
At The Hotel Masson, Veytaux	33

II The Wives

I.	Bound for Keeping	37
II.	The Age	38
III.	Manifest Content	39
IV.	Parturient	40
V.	Liminal	41
VI.	Totals	42
VII.	Ash	43
VIII.	Progenitor	44
IX.	Summering	45
X.	Ipse Dixit	46
XI.	The Muse, marked with 'N'	47
XII.	Out with Men	48
XIII.	Farewell	49
XIV.	Mythologies	50
XV.	Fated	51

III

The Birth   55
Enter Wo   56
Homecoming   57
Conversation Between Daughter and Mother   59
The Reflection   61
Hilltop Mission—Avalon, Catalina Island   62
The Poet   63
Grive Musicienne   64
Varna   65
Taniwha at Whatipu   66
Counsel   67
Her Face, Which Does Not Lie   69
Prayer for Calypso   70
Teeth   71
Continental Typewriter 1927   72
The Maiden of All Desires   73
After Lee Miller's *Exploding Hand*   74
Dada at the Pompidou   75
Rinconia   76
Bain de Pâquis   77
Spider   78
Nation Language   79
The Saltonstall Family   80
Brides   81
Multigravida   82
Umschalter   86
Amanuensis at the Chromatic Gate   87

'A little bloodstained clockwork in a puddle of blood.'
—Peter Redgrove and Penelope Shuttle,
The Hermaphrodite Album

I

Invocation

To be of use, but nothing will decant. Perilous consonant, seized as jewel, betrothed as fire is to the ordinary. A spell; a note. Combatant of will and engraver of sighs. Poultice to the hush, to the whispers of women in corded rooms and to the glows beneath doorways. Purchaser of anointments, slatherer of knives and spoons. Rind of merciless ends and clothier of borrowed aliases. Trenchant penurist, hoarder of silvered lakes. Post chaise bending on the whim of royal deliverance. Coin to whom there is no weight to match the fruit of emptied forest. Animal to cistern, face to coda, god to neither me to neither them, to she. To whom one is infinitely married, and yet cannot be affixed. Enter. All that spills over from my able palm is you.

The Octagonal Tower

'History is the love that enters us through death; its discipline is grief.'
—Anne Michaels

I.

Whatever rage has come through these sealed doors,
and scalded us black and frayed, we have no name for.
We cannot explain the quiet, sleepless shift of whispers,
a procession of shrouds along our corridors,
or the diverted eyes that cloud to see a row of winter oaks outside
shocked in their dendritic fizz. And if we do know it,
it is in the blood, in this terrible synapse of sky, in the road away.
From our house we drive down through a sunken valley
where, like a crypt, it is forever the hour of the dead.

You have always worn the wheel, pushed your hands and wrists
through its axes, as though it were a shackle. Driven, hunched.
It is the same—the sting of yucca and eucalyptus, a vein of pink
bougainvillea purged in hot pulses off rooftops—a fragrant massacre—
and the same steady road you drive every time afraid to speak,
afraid to ask when I will leave you alone in that house with your wife.
I translate your favourite song in my mind: *This song of mine, no one will sing.*
This song of mine that I sing myself will die tomorrow with me.

An October night, 1975. A sudden rain has liquefied the earth.
Mud isn't enough. There is a word you use that means more than mud,
it is the sound of a foot, sunken to the ankle, pulling itself out—
the awful suck of uprooting. Like a scream, it is the fear of standing
so long that you might stay and sink forever. This sound trails
behind you and your brother as you walk the fields one last time.
You will leave and not return for ten years, to marry my mother
who you've not yet met. Your four bare feet make an agreement
with the earth, to remember. It prints its own response in your shadows.

II.

Holidays are uncertain times. The marble face of an old king's grief
deflects the spectacle of his queen's death in each perfect tessera.
The Taj rises above the Jammuna, doubles paradise in the mastery of slaves.

Holidays are uncertain times; their hands are cut off arms thrown up
in celebration. Now they too mourn, and skyward pray to phantom limbs
in the gardens of heaven, alone to pluck and preen.

They are carted away without ceremony, along with the remains of stone
that, like teeth, fall out of swooning heads. The funeral begins.
Mumtaz, hollow as a bride, is veiled in by her white, carved lid.
No one knows when you were born. They think it was an autumn month.
At five you asked where your mother was. Your soot lashes pooled with fear.
Gone to your grandmother's. Later you found her picture—
a woman propped up, freshly dead, her hands emptied of the past.
And you, seated on her lap, two years old, holding her
and what held her forever in that exposure.

III.

The road widens past tracts of arched houses;
you drive faster and grip the wheel.
I say I won't leave till after the New Year,
but by now it doesn't matter.
Your knuckles are bloodless, and your stoic eyes
are the calm surface of a timepiece.

Shah Jehan, imprisoned in a tower by his son,
was sent a gold platter the day of the coup
with the head of his chosen heir upon it.
Seeing this the old king fell, knocked the teeth out of his head.
For eight years he watched the Taj from his window,

from across the river, in a diamond mounted in the wall
that reflected it a million times over.
The soft marble hands of his wife extended to him,
to the empty casket beside her.
When the river filled, he walked across it.

When the door opens, only one of us leaves.
I watch your car until it is far down
through the shadows of trees. The road receives you,
and the house receives you, as does the galley of water,
the trimmed hedge, the cold, sterile cell.

In your wallet, you carry a picture of my mother,
from before my birth, when she was only yours.
Her pinks match the pinks of flowers; she bows her head
into the branch and smiles, as beautiful as a queen.
Love is incidental, time-bound. It is the memory of love we love.
It is the memory that fattens on pain—of these small deaths
and these stone walls. The crown that has sunken from your ears
and hangs around your neck is all that remains.

Archive for a Daughter

November 1972, Derby

A dance card embalmed in sweat.
Her ruthless curve of palm
mowing the carpet into sheaves before a gas fire.

Liquidescent virgin in a purple dress.
Oil paint, shaded avocado, umbrella sun-wings.

Box 2, folder 20 'Early Married Life'

a single page:
  recto
    a fashionable centre-parting
  verso
    consonants: midnight affair nuclear affair bleach affair
  watermark indecipherable

[But here we are jumping ahead]

The archivist notes that no exact birth date is known.
An already Western dressed 6-year-old reads the headlines
of English newspapers for party tricks.
Her black eyes are blunt and unequivocal like the prophecies of pharaohs.
In a Punjabi village, she and her impeccable mother, gemstoned, oracular,
princess a vernal causeway.

Box 1, folder 2 'Emigration'

The BOAC stewardesses Max Factor crinkled baskets
of sweets to soothe the girl's swinging, impatient feet.
Aviation—a risky endeavour in 1963—levels a curse at her progeny.
Aerophobia—her own daughter's—
fear of the air between home and exile collapsing.

Box 1, folder 7 'Education'

Homelands Grammar School For Girls

Miss Moore leans across an oak sea and parquets a line of future mothers.
Her bovine sympathies, neatly pressed, tentacle
                              towards the only Indian in the class.
    The Georgian battlecross marking her forehead,
                              kindly and thoughtfully, segregates.

The girl bounds wildly through the Public Library—
Huxley to her 11-year-old mind suggests individuality—
                    but the Savage's feet recommend no one specific exit.

folders 8–17

Unbound Notebook, mostly unreadable:

*I thought I could become a doctor and asking found I could not think to ask
to become anything*

The archivist notes that these pages are not continuous.
Refer to Box 2, folder 10 'Correspondence'.
A photograph of a prospective husband and several handwritten credentials.

Box 3, folder 1 'Notes on Motherhood'

Nursery—pram—groceries—pram—doctor's visit—
                              cucumbers in half-lengths—
—over each shoulder some conspicuous intellect—

Husband-academic, wife-typist.
    She door-to-doors Hoovers, Avon, thick rosaries of factory lace,
while her children pop tic-tacs for invented ailments in plastic houses.

Nottingham hurls snowballs at her black turbaned gentleman.

Soaked typescript, fair copy of a life—

When she asked her parents for a spare suitcase for an exodus,
   they replied *my child, nothing is ever spare*

Box 4, folder 1 'Exile'

1985, Vancouver—ablaze with cherry blossoms from here to the kindergarten.
We arrived with one steel pot, a bag of lentils and an onion.

   folder 2

1987, North Hollywood—submarine fences root Thanksgiving potatoes, one
a piece. My daughter reads Laura Ingalls Wilder to her menagerie of dolls.
Raft sails calmly on.

   folder 3

1989, Oxnard—Gifted children are purse strings.
We mind their collegiate years with interest.
El Rio wizens to a stockpile of citrus and rental agreements.

   folder 4

1995, Ventura—Bibled to real estate, gold blazers
cinch round a wade of blonde, leathered adulterers.
The neighbours tend their god-plots of lawn and hedge.

Box 5, folder 1 'Drs Parmar'

She saunas with the ladies of the Gold Coast—
   one Japanese ex-comfort woman, one savvy señora
   goldbuckled and multifranchised.

Stanford, Northwestern, Harvard, London, Cambridge—
and when my husband's sisters wept
because I had no sons I said I have two doctors
(one of body, the other of mind)
and sent my uterus via Federal Express
to the village, with my compliments!

On the verso, written in ink, is a page from Box 1, folder 8 [misplaced]

I remember clearly when I knew that I would one day die.
I was on the toilet and I was 11.
The bathroom was white and oblivious.

Recuerdelo

for Parveen

Your word comes back
a caution not to act   after the act

Picking blackberries in Leah's yard
away from her mother
who had locked herself   in the bathroom

We were young and bled easily into incautious hands
the thin-skinned spoils of weeds

In every month there were roses
given women's names
dried in Santa Anas by day   to be laid heavy with dew
at night when they dream   of floating
on seamless lakes   with hands at each sloped bank
that tremble and reach
but cannot break their sleepless sleep

Your word blinks away an ocean through an invisible porthole
It is how we remind ourselves   what does it mean

That secret tongue   impermissible as poverty
the smell of mixed fats frying
of lumbered bellies and their shirts   rising

The eager hands inching up simple and sudden and silent
like the raising   of a dawn-lit window

Against Chaos
after Jagjit Singh

Love could not have sent you, in this shroud of song,
To wield against death your hollow flute, tuned to chaos.

Whatever the Ancients said, matter holds the world
to its bargain of hard frost. But life soon forgets chaos.

He who has not strode the full length of age, has counted
then lost count of days that swallow, like fever, dark chaos.

And you, strange company in the backseat of childhood,
propped on the raft of memory like some god of chaos,

You threaten to drown me: wind through palmed streets.
Oracle of grief. The vagrant dance of figures in chaos

carting trash over tarmac. Stench of Popeye's Chicken,
the Capitol Records building, injecting light and chaos

into the LA sky. That paper boat in rainwater, rushing, dives
out of my reach and old women give no order here to chaos,

nor calm with their familiar tales. Your voice follows me
into and out of the wrong houses, riding my heels in chaos

as if to say that every half-remembered element I've forged
in glass is only the replicate, dying shadow of love's chaos

that once spoken, is like a poison dropped in the mouth
of song, turning it dolorous and black. I've eaten this chaos,

its paroxysm of birth, and seen it uncoil from the faces
of loved ones, into sickness and distance and loss. Chaos

that hounds—that drums its fingers on the window like rain—
who will not forget me and permit me to reach across

thirty years for the child peering out over the very same
landscape, day after day. Yellowing day, that day of chaos

where you are still sounding your warning (though I was too
young). To be left with the bitter heaviness of song, its chaos.

June 16, 1956. The Church of St. George the Martyr

It will be fifty years soon.
And yet it seems the preparations have not begun,
for there are still thoughts of winter
in the boughs above Queen Square.

A drake flies overhead. I think he is lost.
His cry is like a man who is to wed.

And what a day it must have been,
the stones of the old church have not forgotten,
though the preparations for your wedding
do not feel as though they have begun.

And yet too late, and so, too late,
the couple that hurries in through the parish gate
welcomes the spirits in empty pews that are to be
their only guests. So, it is the same as it was then.

But it is not the same and yet it is, time will make
much of this and much of you and yet it cannot be the same.

A man, bustles into the square in a black raincoat
like someone in a scare, frightens the cashmere
gentlemen that back away from him
and his immortal packages. In each arm he carries ten
or more Styrofoam boxes labelled 'human organ'
and runs and runs, hoping to arrive before the knowledge
of their death blackens the skins of his beating carriage.

The preparations have arrived and gone.
We hustle the dead around and imagine
somehow that they are alive, that time could still ferry you
back and transplant you untarnished in this beginning.

The sky is late, later than it was fifty years ago that day
when you, having married, were carried out hurriedly
in something pink and knitted with one summer rose,
that blossomed in your hand in Bloomsbury on Bloomsday.

Newnham Portraits

'The unmarried and childless cut themselves loose from racial immortality, and are dedicated to individual life—a side track, a blind alley, yet surely a supreme end in itself.'
—Jane Ellen Harrison, *Reminiscences of a Student's Life* (1924)

Blanche Athena   sibylous   congestive
    foursquares her fairshare
                at the garden party of 1921.

Note the three white buttons of her white-buttoned coat
    so bald and yet so *intime*.

    Four decorous maenads sweep arm-in-arm across the lawn.
                Discarded theories swarm in their wake.

       Athena   whatever in you spins, drying its lips,
    dies here at the feet of your mistresses.

Hope Mirrlees in Cyrillic veil
    manstands to outfoot the Reverend Stewart,
        a hypertrophic rhododendron.
    The Reverend withers.

Lady Gladstone extends a satin hand, as if to say
    'I do not mind if nothing comforts me'.

The Clough Gates, embattled, unhinged,
        excise like a pastry knife the suitors' ambitions,
       who smoke, smugly Edwardian,
           grimacing like very polite steam engines.

A Bengali couple (unidentified), reluctantly caught in black and white,
    what a damned waste all this must have seemed to them—
    they, who came only by invitation—
    unplaceable now, wiped from the college register.

As out of place as locusts,
        as the *fin-de-siècle* fad for green dresses,
        as Morris's paper Pomegranates and Virginia Creeper.

The wife's discomfited glare
        pleads as she pulls from the frame, knowing that
the complexity of the individual spells death.

Note: The bronze gates of Newnham College, the 'Clough Gates', were badly damaged in 1921 when a group of male undergraduates tried to smash their way into the college with a coal trolley. The boys were celebrating after the Senate had voted against admitting women to full membership of the University of Cambridge.

Chopin's Waltz No. 7

The Classics contrabanded in the cellar with rose petal jam.
(Rose petal jam?) A week of breakfasts' invisible guest.
Husbands and fathers, too, ghosted every meal.
You were their substitute, rationed nephew, the favourite.

Feline cousins, Deanna and the other (what was her name?
Imagine Helen of Troy, only topless and more petulant)
each claimed an arm. Above ground, Tanti Ani boudoired
all day in a fuss with curlers and romance novels.

At dinner, she thumped the table and shouted, 'Rachmaninov!'
The stuffed peppers swallowed their tongues, the mish-mash
glistened indifferent. You rose, cigaretted, rolled your sleeves,
patterning clouds with your teeth into notes in the air.

Ani forgot her communist meanness, her housedress, her wigged
ugliness. (Where had her husband gone?) Partnered alone
to Chopin's No. 7 (*Walzen* is to roll, revolve, to shove blame),
she debutanted like a Hapsburg princess in a scandaled room.

Tempo cut slow enough to let the mind finger its black stakes
back, mindful not to displace the past, the relics of conspiracies,
black lists, shots to the temple. She could have hanged herself
and swayed, smiling for you who never wanted to leave.

Loy Returns to Paris

Le Bonheur   the bloodless mechanics of travel.
Kicking at space is no arrival.

You collect the child you left   now provincial
and round   from planning menus and improving her script
for four years in an Italian village.
Giulia's *negrita Joella*, her
curls browning illegitimately.

The rue Campagne-Première,   a grey, hutched widow-latch
for a Poiret with fine bone structure.

Refurbished vanities choir on workshop tables.

Address books somersault, and a life is written
from 'Z' to pseudonym.

Curving fingers smelt graphite into cracks.   Fine noses
of inherited genius,
blackly spar and bring turtles
to your babies,   note their approving babble
for use in their trades.

Elbowed pages, snapped under books, crooked
deletions migrate   in the direction of an echo.
Festooned shadows bend over your youngest

Fa bene, dusting pillboxes, carrying coloured glass
from one childhood to the next.

Tartarus

after Ovid's Heroides VII

Palmed over   queen of Carthage
    To be written on   those flanks glassed by fire

Genius dips a pen in his own vitreous humour   a blind epic, blindly
        scribed
cock-archer   with excellent penmanship   guards his muscleisms

Dido   plait your several complaints   from which to swing
holophone to history   wife   wanderer

    The lot that was mine in days past still follows me in these last moments

blood-slipping at your altars   your memory pyre   a temple

The tabernacle swallows the choir

voices disperse   like obsolete coins   like the syncopations of cowards

and yet—   in hell   —the poets say, she would snub him!

Childed woman, child   neithered by death
who painted her collars in chloroform
who pocketed basalt

who measured out those words   to be sung by the white swan
    by the shallows of Meander: *lacrimis ultima*

Ambracia
after Ovid's Heroides XV

The Fates unthimble   call   Hell-witch   Hell-suitor
      I burn—as burns the fruitful acre.

Four hundred years too late
Esurient elegists   swing platters round a famine

Still   your orphan glues her tongue in place
refusing marriage.   Hell-dog   Hell-widow—

Suicided fragments   befit your escape.
How you wombed yourself   to failure

            and rolled off Leucadia
In a black wedding hymn.

Hell-lyre   Hell-mother   *My craft is not impelled.*
No womanly contest.   The empty coverlet concludes   your death, sexless

your apologies, mortal.   No night cry   no monument
      no sermon   to unlock those cusped ovations

but the wave
      that anchors its testimony to the white, inviolable air.

Ephyre
after Ovid's Heroides XII

Oathed to silence   the choral tongues   a propitious alloy
whose valence darkens like a bandage.   Pity, that Argo
          pulled by Hera's net   could not be persuaded into death
(the anointed shoal   had been wetted and fed)
                    pity, also
                    that tragedy   foresworn   belies the trial.

Goddess of the Crossways   Priestess of Hecate   Queen of Colchis—
     your phylogenies of grief   each absolute as woman's rule
          even gods would not intervene.

          Of the deed my right hand was bold enough to do, it is not bold
                    enough to write.

Your dowry   unclaimed   rises from your native shore
          purples your exilic robes.   Niece of Circe
Granddaughter of Helios—

     My ire is in travail with mighty threats.

Such labours   to unhusband   to unmother   to reverse
     the plough of bronze-footed bulls
          to refleece the golden sheep.

Medea   your famed barbarity   drives pins in the specimen
                    diagnosed   individual
                                       (motherhood is fatal)

Chorus:
          [Strophe:] Through each name laughter
                    waves its emphatic emblem.
          [Antistrophe:] What culpable orchestration!

The White Sister

The white sister   tithes her purloined sainthoods
and orders her chalk menagerie   into face supplanting face

They are   that is
umbilical favours   discoloured by debt   transposed onto your name

Family   to whom one is infinitely wived

Sea-house on a molten shore   where always
you age in half-life   live   as a child might

without dowry or brother   husband or defect   the sister

floats farther into that silvered catacomb   that avowed promontory
between daughter and daughter

Beatified

on the accordance of India's first female saint

The elders   the traders   make their calculations—
how to protocol an empty seed   how to domain thirty inches
      of black hair?

Sister Alphonsa   disfigures herself into their   sum total
burns   femur, buttocks
      shipping her smouldered arc towards god

with a bell-pull   a black band   and a christening gown.

Ladies   your order   the Poor Clares
touch toe to heel   washed by your burial.
    Where you   rapiering that birthright to bear nothing
intoned:

    Ganymede pull your oxen—

and alight! The paralysed boy twitches a devotional
      for Thomas Aquinas.

Suffer is the hilt
    is the enterprise.

But to suffer   differently   for the white-scarred marriage
for the light fabling in the theatres of mortals—
      for this that is only so female—

your lock-lust geometries   shall not be pardoned.

At the Hotel Masson, Veytaux

Aberrant en Suisse   Montreux perils for a verdict
violets and pinks   indiscriminate and ruched as Alps
parasol along the Quai des Fleurs. The lake, like so much else,
is inevitable   it shudders in its vernal collet
with the persistence of a coquette   banging her head
noiselessly and determinedly against that clock which never skips nor
        slows—breath, mot juste,
deportment, please.

        Savoyard topiaries   Chillon, a réchauffé in kidskin.
Byron and Shelley are upstaged—
enter from the rue Bonivard a BMW two-seater   in speed
the piratical midnighters, exigent, off-colour
we flee to our hotel balcony, upper circle.

An idolatry of wood shutters   medieval keyholes   burnt out crosses.
        Madame has a lovely trout on her face   and is so decent.
Her and the maid (now waitress)
thumb a potage of sparrowgrass on our brows.
                A duck floats on sauce miel, unfooted, clean at the neck.

Such an ecclesiastical pair   our witnesses   stoic and reverent
and rehearsed   and the maid
a bright, terrible thing   laughing   polluting the dining room
        from behind a cloth screen.
She and Madame share a joke (a kiss?) a tale   *elle est très jolie!*
        A romance   ours   cools on its dish.

        The girl slides a gateau between us   bows, is repealed, wants applause.
Dent du Midi, an affair in vanilla cream
                manifold of peace   in terra impasse.
        An entire nation   secured from all sides by meringues.
                Her infatuate smile discharges in your hand
                and is without antidote.

II

The Wives

'Black seed of the old man,
Why did he have to marry.'
—James Tate, 'The Old Man's Young Wife'

I. Bound for Keeping

Older Wife   most trusted specimen, good for
              jimmying jam jars and prophesying the arrival of the post
but not for cartwheel exploitations via laundry basket, which was once
     her forte but, alas, now is not.

Yet how many ailments had she squinted at and advanced towards healing?
     Even her daughters   a little older than the new wife
had renounced their fleshly bond   blank at the sight of her

like freshly-ironed citizens
              roaming the suburbs   in post-menstrual exile.

All that day-glo money and beauty   who could have predicted?

But everything points to my not being here, she said.

              When he told her he was bringing home a younger wife
                            her heart tore itself into tiny pieces.

II. The Age

It is lately the age for such things.

The new wife troubles herself with arching—
                      brows, leg, hips, back—

so many arches are hubris for any façade
            a necessary mastery for

the emperor who, parading through,
                              mints his profile, laurels his generals.

Older Wife fans out a deck of cards and selects her seven suitors,
            smokes, goes outside, waits.

The lamplight throws itself against the shadowed walls of her
            husband's bedroom
                        like the burning of so many cities.

III. Manifest Content

What do you think it means, she asks.

The new wife, awoken by a bleeding suit of armour, is licking the ends
of her hair.

The kitchen's muscular smell is making her sick.   *But what does it mean?*
She dangles at the doorway, refusing to enter.

Older Wife squats over a bowl of potatoes,
balding its contents blind and limbless.   *Fertility*, she replies.

IV. Parturient

As for her own dreams, Older Wife was wise enough to forget them.

Watching the dew round and swell in the early light made her ache

an ache she remembered from her childhood—

mad cell split of one mind forcing its way around a point so small

that it made the universe distend and choke, distending. She gripped

the sink cold and hard and further out she could hear the engines spin

inside an oak gall and her ears were filled with the anger of bees.

V. Liminal

What custom brings you here? She thought, but did not say.
    Her husband's ancestral retinue
shuffle past her without a word.

    New Wife greens, glasses, retches, sleeps.
                  And who could not admire her?

An earthen jug is passed
        from the mouth of one to the next to the next and to the hands of
                Older Wife who is bent over the fire.

A plague of aunties hibble and hex.

Why should our brother be blessed with a son?
        They sour the butter in the churn. Their husbands
                tuck their prayer beads into their shirts.

    Older Wife singes her sleeve, some would say, by accident.

VI. Totals

No matter how she divides her sums some fraction remains.

    The New Wife is a balled integer and the light gestates
        about her bedroom, oily as a housefly.

Older Wife brings in a tray of something glutinous.
    How fat she is   *and what a lazy temperament*

Her black hair vegetates a grammar of coils—the pillow's hieroglyphs—
    which Older Wife decodes.

    The body's memory, thickened in each prurient strand—

a husband's excess, a wife outstripped and these curved arrows that diverge
    to kill one and appoint another.

Each hair a forgery of another love   so multiple, so numerous, so febrile
    that Older Wife presses them between her palms
    and smothers their cries.

VII. Ash

I am being poisoned, the New Wife declares one morning that had been, thus far, unremarkable.

The husband looks up from his plate, opens his mouth, lowers his eyes, gets up to leave.

The two wives sit over identical teacups in silence.

VIII. Progenitor

June dragged the loudest screams across the house.

The child was undeniable and made rotund gestures.

      Quick-footed doctors flew in circles around the maternal bed

making the waxwork breathe.

The New Wife   loosened from her orbit   reeled and wobbled

    sinewed to her fruit.

        The husband   broad and delicate   fleshed himself a new axis.

IX. Summering

Older Wife buttons herself on the Metro. She was not always so husbanded.

Fine proxies of joy revisit her in these hours between the growing of milkteeth.

An evening revivifies—when her words

    dropped from heaven's collate beams of amber—

    and she, by an Alpine lake, picnicked on a vertiginous rouge

    and said something like 'isn't the water so clear' and all was at once still

    and reconciled to the choiring of her own voice with the ageless mountains.

X. Ipse Dixit

And when she looked up again the trees had thinned and the water
　　　was consoling itself under ice.

Older Wife had been watching the boy-child trump his mother
　　　wherever her foot fell.

But what was she reading? Behind a curtain, the New Wife was unfolding
　　　envelopes and photographs and red scented paper.

Look at this! she hissed.

　　Blonde all blonde all teeth all nails all cabaret all orifice all severance—
　　　　hurtling towards them with her Weimar collarbones.

XI. The Muse, marked with 'N'

Enter daughter of memory   whose alkaline tongue ripples the shore
of another life.

The Danube, lipsticked to an average intellect and curls of hair—

His exploits were not always so cerebral.

Husband fettered a half-inch of every perfume to his account book
    and tabulated that Older Wife
        her phlox   her oxides   her fuss
no longer inspire.

    Alight!   Boiling feldspar to an aqueous preciosity, the New Wife
is some experiment   and the Husband, a Chemist of fine nostrils.

Narcissus, alchemical, wanders every which way in cashmere and cigarettes

      (and the pocket frays where Older Wife mended it)

making invisible sighs   consulting the biographies of great men
pocketing the chamois of some sick and feral creature for an antidote to love

      Are the laws of the heart so simple?

Older Wife has seen these daughters wave their braceleted arms
    and steal her Husband ashore.

XII. Out With Men

Older Wife could only imagine

how they troubled themselves with the thoughts of men.

How her husband, buoyed by talk of other women,

procured drink and lost centuries to the likes of Coleridge,

who (albeit clever) suspended parental rights,

absconded and left his child to die

(where his wife discarded the infant's yardage of muslin, its baptismal yoke,

was, to Coleridge, a mystery of his birth).

XIII. Farewell

New Wife would not bolt   and what a disaster
          when her half-clean notes fell even below sound
the child, too, went quiet.

She sleeps pincushioned to the marital bed, now empty.

          Older Wife carries in a tray of dates   boiled insects.

Husband returned at dawn for his flask and turned on his heel
          for the reek was too much.

The bedroom would not pipe up to the equivocal noises of birds
          and the earth was hard.

XIV. Mythologies

How calming   the humming of a woman   kitchened by circumstance
            dispersed from herself by routine.

New Wife emerges from her sleep
            pitching thorns, sharp like the spires of cathedrals,
                                    from her hair

Older Wife is perched over the stove's inevitable plane
        over refusals to eat   and cold ornaments   she cannot master.

New Wife rotates a glass of water with one hand,
expressing a wish to travel.

XV. Fated

If she had been scattering anything in order to collect it later,
whatever order she imposed she admired alone.

    Even the cards—their concomitance—would not intercede.

    Several silences conspire to bring about her life.

And the scroll on the lap of the High Priestess would not,
by her own fallow hand, unroll.

III

The Birth

I am full of it   the love you crammed down my throat.
          I am about to explode.
You stretch on your plastic gloves
     move about, aiming to catch it.   I am tight as a drum for now.
There are movements   within me—winged roads   to paradise.

It will come out like shrapnel.

The sun is jet, and shadows
glow like hot stones.   We pose for now
          in the brilliant act of happiness.
This death is enviable.   It is the only truth we will ever know—
these secrets   fly   no longer our own.

Enter Woe

'Woe is the one who, languishing, waits for her lover.'
—'The Wife's Lament', *The Book of Exeter*

The shadow of a blackbird
falls across her path.

It is not an omen—
but whatever is the exact opposite.
Three tin wheels push over it,
steadied by two skinny legs.

The sun's dark tendon
watches, then alights.

Woe hears her mother calling.
The tricycle twists
and wobbles into the garden,
pining and rattling.

Homecoming
after Christa Wolf's Cassandra

Voices spear the darkness. Troy is no more than the glint
of departing soldiers. We pass in and out of smoke.

Soon, it is morning. It is not morning.
The false night of forensic lamplight is the dawn.

A distant wood reflects, thick with torsos blaring white,
and hands raise, empty on the approaching shore, to deny.

The light accuses every surface. All are mute:
thorns and swollen lips stiffen the undergrowth.

I am Cassandra, née Iphigenia, Cassandra, née Iphigenia.
I have exited time, prophet and sacrifice, to speak.

Don't you recognize me? This face is the same.
Time bears the burden of my many names.

Through the trees, on a field, sheep appear to kiss the earth
but aren't. They tear it up between their teeth.

The sea is as good as an oracle, she has brought me back
and forth, her waves equivocate with bound wrists.

Sails slip from their poles and collapse too weak to weep,
like slave women, who do not tell what they have seen. But I have seen

my city's walls blown through with greed, I have seen its faces sicken,
black with fear—and fear, I've seen it sicken faster into death, have seen it—

seen each of my sisters' blood thicken; I have seen its impure colour
sweeten altars, dragged through graves, to be silenced again and again,

seen the kings and seen the princes, seen the howl of death
and its advances—clattering thousands in helmets and skulls and ears,

and it has not silenced me. I am free. You will undo me
with the stab of revenge—that has wounded only my dreams, till now.

I catch sight of you, and you are watching me, noble and cold as victory.
Father, our weary king, steps from the ship into your marble arms.

Mother it is me—don't you recognize me? I am Cassandra, née Iphigenia,
Cassandra, née Iphigenia. Take me to you, and I am home.

Take me to your smooth, perfumed shoulders, to your grieving mask,
and I am you, you—you come back to you.

Conversation Between Daughter and Mother
after Paula Rego's Convulsion

I. Celestina

I am nearly done laying you out. Because you are still alive
you will not think I have done it with tenderness.

But there are no bruises, and no seams to reveal where I,
cataloguing your smells, shelled you out of your skin,

that shroud belonging now to me. It must be said,
you were faultless as a god,

your lunar voice warm against my forehead,
as the fruit from your marble orchard.

This time, it is I who elevate you over a pool of water,
thumbing your eyes shut.

This time I am your mother and it is I who will decide
when you are clean. Blank as you are,

I assume your pure skin, marked
by illness, by memory.

I have painted the walls with my image of you,
your face may be yours, but it is my mask, into which I have cut

these numerals for smiles, these words
in blood   I have made them hard not to notice.

It is a privilege, as much as it is your curse, to have found myself
alive inside you, to snap each precious chord

each belt-wire, each acid corpuscle, to hear them fizz regret
for not begging me to stop   for not letting me kill you sooner.

II. In Extremis

With a single cry, you recoil from me for the second time
seeing this body, so contemptible, so feeble. You deny me
thinking perhaps that you are able, thinking in fact that I am evil.

Here are several others, here are witnesses   anxious, severe
waiting to hear you screaming. This time it is you who will do
the naming, and I who will be swathed and laid out for your keeping.

Daughter, this body will grow more and more familiar. The mirror
you have hung with that little girl forever in it will slowly accept
my image, black-clothed, vampiric.   Do not be frightened.

It is not for you that I am dying, or for myself that I am weeping.
Like the first time you are so clever to be reborn of my leaving.
Return to me once more and receive your mother   Lamia, Gello.

Drink this poisonous pity. Let this woman carry you off your chair.
She is not a maid, but a midwife. She will help you forget,
she will help you suckle. These common oracles with their common miracles!

She offers condolences and tidies up the ossuary; she is off to ring the bells.
After so many years, drink, innocent and eager.
My love is endless. All I have left to give you is blood.

The Reflection

This light blunts your imperfections—
you are my shadow, prim and desperate.
The fountain bleeds sympathy,
sputtering iodine over the shoal, the keloid face
of a life shelled too quickly. I stare into it;
it has nothing to do with me. It is unnatural,
the heavy glare so slow, the stone
under the pour of water, so stupidly effaced.
But you and I are one, rooted in some obscene fact.
The water regurgitates its own spill, as if to correct.

Hilltop Mission—Avalon, Catalina Island

In a dream, she holds a mirror
between her fingers   pared to white.
Advancing towards my bed   she turns to where I lie

Glass and bone click   the slowing of blood marks the minute
in seconds   an organ abandoned, the mirror rises.
I cannot wake   we press our lips to the reflection
La Malinche.

A Spaniard, cuckold to time,
fingers his golden watch   to praise the woman
moored at his side   for the red, split tongue
that felled her people.

Love dies fast over four hundred years
of following husbands   to new nations
to be made heroines   and to learn the language of confession
that haunts these tubular halls of blood.

We followed them to the font   to the baptismal
and there we drowned our children;
there we flashed that immortal smile hidden by flesh
in which we will unknowingly   receive judgment

Father, in all your grace   shave our heads
and leave us on the mission steps   to wail
and hold our rag corpses those babies we never let be born

We ripped open their soft throats
and there   just under the skin as you said   were the colours
of our disease.

The Poet

Your love will not make me forget her   she sits, winding
her black umbilicus   that disastrous cord   waiting.

I have told you only today   I see her
just now at our table   her formalin skin slack and dark

her hair brittle, tinctured with musk   and rage.
She is the full possessor   of oblivion   an alternative

to your eternity   happiest, happiest.
You think if you are quiet she will leave.

The door opens—
what you can't see   this shadow   I am bound to

approaches.   Her liquefaction, a poultice for the infinite
we correspond, we correspond.

Her spate, reeling
into the dark.   I have stayed away too long

it is only a matter of time
till she takes me back.

Grive Musicienne

We lean into the sun, finding our reflections
inside coffee cups, on windows, the slant of the roof
and the clouds that, like an eagle, push off the Alps
and ascend into heaven.

Below, a song thrush flies up to each windowpane
and carries on bolting and rushing for some time,
brushing its brown belly on the smooth glass.

Last night I told you that my favourite colour was red,
but there is no red out of our window today,
so it has ceased to be my favourite. Instead I have taken yours:
yellow, for these pots of braying daisies, for this light
that fades when it touches your golden skin and pales.

The bird, silent now, marches towards its other
in the mirror, wings aloft, and fails and fails.

Varna
after Sappho, Fragment 6

So

       this is the sea you have been carrying.

       I should have known it
       by the sound,
       when I tip your heart to my ear,
       how it claims to take me.

Go   my beloved,
So we may see if I hunger after it.
       Potentate of dreams,
       lady

of gold arms, of wide sweeping folds and salt weeds.
       She has pocked the earth blind with her shattered octagons.
       The sand bears her longing, that
doom
       of intermittent love.

Taniwha at Whatipu

'…I remember the bay that never was
And stand like stone and cannot turn away.'
　　　　　　　　—James K Baxter, 'The Bay'

Fiesome and button-gunny　　　　the awed tailors
chew their needles　　to see you borne out, weathering for beauty.

This is hard-earned sibilance.
The earthly mantle that comes with a hero's death.

The chorus mares its black singing.　　　　From the shore
white-hearted celibates　　　　　line up like tall breakers

crown for the pearls you hang in each ear.
The moon as celebrant divides the remaining hours into loaves,

makes oaths of stone as women do.

Counsel

for Anna Smaill

Looking to ward off danger, I browse the eighth floor of the Bobst Library
    for some composite rite,
a wrist-length of red thread,
    éblouissements to blind intervening shadows.

*

It is good luck to dream of your wedding day,
to feed a cat from an old shoe (so long as the cat does not sneeze).
Do not marry a man born in the same month as you,
or eat while dressing. Tear your veil (at the altar by accident).
Wear earrings. Not pearls. Carry salt. Drink water.

Beware a woman carrying an empty bucket.
Turn away from the mothers of stillborn sons, monks, pigs and lizards.
Under no circumstances should you marry on a Tuesday. Or Thursday.
And once you start from home, don't dare to look back.

*

How to coin the finest and most singular antidote—
to dance against possible risk?

From PR6003.U64—
the fair-weather lesbians of Dorothy Bussy's *Olivia*—
to the *Diary of Virginia Woolf: 1915–1919* [PR6045.072]
we plunge straight into Lily the 'simple-hearted' servant, her indiscretions.
A married Miss Stephen keeps schtum
in her tremorous florals two sizes too big.

Zigzagging to PR4863.A33 *The Letters of Charles and Mary Lamb*:
'Your goose found her way into our larder with infinite discretion.
Judging by her Giblets which we have sacrificed first,
    she is a most sensible Bird.'
[C.L. to John Rickman, 30 December 1816]

At PR4231.A43: *Robert Browning and Elizabeth Barrett: the courtship
    correspondence—*
Nuances of love and outrage elongate a shortened life.
I drift towards one leaning oversize *Wandering of the Soul* [PJ1551.E3];
Egyptian Papyri transmuted into spells for safe passage in the afterlife.
'Do not stop to play draughts with the Dead
lest you be trapped for eternity.'

To the Brothers Grimm [PT921.K56]—
Three women turned into identical flowers in a field.
Only one returned home every night. At dawn she said to her husband:
'If you come this morning and pick me,
I shall be set free and stay with you forever.'
Imperative chance. He chose correctly.

       *

Dearest one, the riddle of marriage admits no luck.
What it recognises is pure—
it fires the dew from sleeping grasses.

Only know that he will not err (and nor will you) where love
has paused in an evening's silence to light the unlit road.

Her Face, Which Does Not Lie

Porcelain is the colour of her skin.
It is also other things entirely.
How to reconcile this fact? It is impossible
to forget that she too was other things.
Who was this vessel
and what made him drink?
Was it the spirit of that river
it is a wonder anyone can remember?
Its name must have been written
by one who, like a jealous wife,
covets the photograph of her husband's mistress.

In German, the word *Porzellan*
does not sound like something
that could be easily broken.
Nor does it seem fitting that such a thing
should lay between two people
who sit together in silence at a table
considering its many other meanings.

'Names are memories of things',
the wife reminds him.
But he remembers differently and so
every now and again when she is alone
she holds the photograph up to the light
to test the quality of her suspicions.

Prayer for Calypso

Marigold at the spindle   cut thrice,
        a triptych of immutable colour.

Curl your dishonoured robes.   Leave off and do not weave your
shadows of laughter, nor trace its naked light.

        Even if your orange hair plaits itself in his dreams,
my hand bore the wave that knelt along the seafloor
        and drove his keel homewards.

Swallow your consonants; they are thin as perfume. As lipstick. As praise.
Be left to reflect, as vanity, your ambivalence. Its own cruel country.

Teeth

In sleep he leaves her. The radio on the sill too is insomniac, blinks through to the glow of hard surfaces, the close walls, the unshaded bulb. All this is corseted in by fire escape and brick, by a dither of jazz and the sudden slap of a report, talk of war. He sleeps still. Fetches breath too fast to calm her. But now, she can see him clearly, through the slick sodium drip from 83rd street. A piano can be heard through the floorboards on which they lie, as though underwater. She cannot be sure, but when the playing stops, cards shuffle. It is too late to be gambling for money, she knows this, and the pianist knows this and so it is not for profit that the suits, light and dark, foretell the next chord. The reporter's voice again disrupts. It is a hard thing, to know the whole world is not sleeping. The man wakes momentarily. He aims an eye at the clock wearily, thinking there'll be time for this tomorrow, for the gnash of uncertain threats. She listens. Waits for the music to start again anywhere. What sleep doesn't see in the dark is still true. The egg crate mat wedged into a corner, the empty cigarette box lying on its own open jaw. The pianist touches the lower keys somehow more severe. The girl loves coincidences. Loves the stack of silk shirts his mother bought and that he wears them. Glares sadly at Modigliani's photograph, at the paints there aren't room enough for that are boxed up like good linen. She herself hardly fits. She turns. A cold wine glass rolls into her back. And boxes that have nowhere to unpack themselves, casually stare at the mess of thrown off clothes. On the dresser there are folded pocket scraps, a single key and the hollow sound of its teeth. He breathes unsteadily into the morning, when he will lean over and ask her how she slept, raise up the curtain and show her the tree outside she might have missed, bronzing the street. When he will see colour. And she will see time.

Continental Typewriter 1927

Bisecting France overnight   First Class
the pull of Paris   apothecary crosses   their blind, green plastics
      space   moves
bunk-strapped   *j'ai*
Ich darf   *glauben*   *das freut mich*
       Was hast du gesehen
l'autre   *im Glas*   *vin de ma patience et perdition*

You might still be there   on platform 16 at the Hauptbahnhof
in your regalia

  *

I brought only what I could leave
    You spread our photographs on a wooden table   light a cigarette
the fountain in the Platz below   only weeps in summer
not November   when it washed fingerprints off my legs and arms

The typewriter you carried from the flea market
for me   you understood why I had to have it
you too the lover of unused things
who forgot to mark the box FRAGILE
its jaw hangs silent at my desk

The Maiden of All Desires

after Federico García Lorca's 'School'

Shipstalled and gesturing   how unclean, your versions of delight.
Midnight to always, foursquare ego   you row athletic
past squiring delicates   with flowers for fools' ruffs

Out to Nordic stars   heavy of art and flesh.
Whirlwinds of gold and maps superimposed   are nothing
to whom nothing belongs   to she who is married to nothing.

Desperate scavenger   folding wives into nameless octavos
for spendthrifts.   The maiden's blue curtain is armless and headless.
To be drawn is her only purpose.

After Lee Miller's *Exploding Hand*

Baleful and proud, the vanity of all that is hers.
      The modern woman—a hand explodes.
Do not touch that which is rumoured to prolonged suffering.
High-wire disembark   coolly suspicious   she trades each paranoia
On the prelude of undoing.   The hand would be perfect if not
For the herald   poled to her fourth digit
abortive in its roundness.

Would it surprise you to know that on reaching the door
she had thought to open it.

Mixing curatives, withed   and wide-eyed
Knowing that only when the moment has come, has it passed.

Dada at the Pompidou

Wo ist Dada? Ist da, da, da. In Paris,
a child's hobbyhorse spins in the air,
lonely, amateurish,
extending its ego in autistic egressions.

Die Ausstellung—
Le moment à venir—

O Mother of the World,
you sit cross-legged with your mandolin
and a brown scarf tied about the chin.

Your noise invites coins;
the rain flecks oracles
into daring pronouncements.

At the entrance
under umbrellas, we listen to your Montenegrin fingers
bow strings as if you were grating nutmeg,

food of prophets.
The brasseries are *Vendredi*-ing,
our *cahiers* sigh at the sight.
In minutes we are all as black as you.

Rinconia

'brackets imply a free space of imaginal adventure'
        —Anne Carson, Introduction to *Fragments of Sappho*

Thought persists toward language

fledge-heeled harmonics glare and punctuate:

      Fragment 87b

          ]anxiety
          ]ground

      Fragment 87c

          ]
          ]daring

600 BC, a brave millisecond.

Mnemosyne cuts out her lashes from the same tree

that spokes the torture wheels of hell.

          You blush redcurrant and descend as you must

artillerist, barren woman

               turning, and then turning to again.

Bain de Pâquis

Fire-yield geometrics ash,
caved into element by element.

Those hoary wires tipped together
scatter a tutelage of solute and air.

In the shade of Mont Blanc, heiresses
unloose knots onto bronzing vertebrae.

Turn back. Air your hot Victorian skirts.
Creation dissipates from its pupilar lacunae.

There I would float, a clavicle
among a row of mirrored swans.

Spider

Black and unkeeping   our futurologist wastes her tongue,
        and lays her orphaned, silvered sack against the door.

Praise her
and her mitred carriage.

Inside their puparium, her charges gloat like hot loaves of hair and pupil.

    What she sees
is laughter squaring out trapdoors on the lawns of undiminished love.

There is no simple rule—   *but man must have his appetites.*
        This fact dies into her proud ornament   of mists and glass.

Nation Language

Maybe it is something to be pitied
like lizianthus in Arab heat…
or listened to like a dark-handed
calypso and then agreed upon in
robed council, smoked in a hookah,
exhaled to distill, imperfect from men's mouths.

* 'Nation Language' is a term coined by Kamau Brathwaite to describe that
language which emerges in a colonialist setting from the submergence of a
mother tongue by the conqueror's language.

The Saltonstall Family

The prolonged façade   of velvet bedcurtains   pinafores and sleeves
    matched by the mother   who is matched to the task of dying
and father—careless reprobate in black—severs the picture.

The elder sister fastens the younger by the wrist, warns
do not interfere   with the red and white of it.

One intimacy too many—
    the glove their father drops into his own mother's pale hand.
It oils.

Father's hat is what will disturb the girl in later years   it is too large
and this will trouble her   the way the dead woman should

The way the too stiff baby in her mother's arms should
The way the certitude of family portraits should,

unpicking themselves in airless rooms.

Brides

Lace anemones   unnoose the hatch
from which life dins   determinedly from its faucet.

Their children sail into the world
                    equinoctial and warlike
                                ankles keeled in arterial blood.

And mothers stride into the nursery from which they crawled,
        summoned by encores.

Gone is the woman and her baby wife
                whose arms are tucked in sleep.

Gone is the full red flush of her
                perambulating in a high-windowed room.

Multigravida
for Parveen

Old woman, old mother—white nucleus

                                    incerebrate in your chair—

the price of cruelty is sacrifice. Repent. Or put away your pearls and scarves.

       Toothless grand-mère—we capsize at your tidal axis.

Your son, a sort of Paris,

    contemplates an apple, split open, hotwires each slumberous lobe.

Its cranial juices electrify. He feeds memory—that grievous syrup—

to his wide-eyed Helen in teaspoons.

Tempts her from coma with its immortal seed.

Prima-mater   Great-matter   your narratives enslave—

        Epic vanity—at such a premium!

At birth your name meaning the 'absolute best'

    was made ordinary by marriage.

        (What husband could outwit such prospects?)

Your daughters run to the temple to pour an impossible bath

    into a leaking vessel.

§

G1P1   (elderly gravida)

Cleopatra eloping through a three-storey window rots on the vine

    in nurses' housing. Struck off the family register

she peddles her blush pigmata (in a fuss of black leather)

    half-wisdoms paling at her mother's locked stare.

Do you remember us all running up the stairs and never saying why?

She husbands a bumbling anglo-bolus whom her father can all but swallow.

G3P2102
Having mastered the rhetorical compliment at a young age
      she vivisects her ego hourly before the mirror—

forgetting her forced cure for pre-martial morning sickness
    or that pell-mell in Las Vegas, jellying in the Mojave sun.

Her twin Samsons raise their jeweled kirpans to proud ovations
    from bearded uncles: *Raj Karega Khalsa*
                (the rest of you can go to Hell).

Am I ugly?

Daemon Beauty whines at her bedside in long gray plaits—
    a ghost of an ancestor steps easily into her, reeks of dry burial
    of fingers around neck sores of unscattered bones.

G2P2
The martyr-mystic   with holy-water cosmetology
wrinkles sincerely over Bollywood soap operas
    believes they are *true stories*
        that every tree trunk on every Indian plain secrets a hoard
            of costume changes.

Complexion monastic
Intellect simple

She adulterates with a radio DJ   falls hard for ad breaks
stirring her tea with a long-distance arranged marriage.

Romeo FM impales himself on her pure white promise
    alone in the sepulchre.

    Dusting for prints   her husband tears open her homespun
    and inflicts her with children.

She dons her new habit with conviction.
     Her house is spotless.
She garlands each of the ten gurus on her knees.

§

God in her own image   grandmother
     meets Lord Krishna.
He presses a diamond into her forehead   they levitate.

     At the door   a half-light of her husband
          death's hallucinogen
               will not enter the house. She waves
and passes him chocolates through the letterbox.

Grand misery   grand hope   grandeur
     she insists on pre-Partition castles and the ownership of one giant
          cannon.
Within the walled city of Sodhra (a hundred doors)
               that trunk of ancestral gold, entrusted to a servant,
          is as bright now as it was to a precociously greedy child.

§

Something has left this house. The bill has been paid.

§

It took grandfather's death to bring us to the source, or so they say, of it.

An animal skin   curdling black in an attic room
     a gift from a wandering sage. The gift of pure vision.

Alone on the tiger skin, grandmother quietly rose inches off the floor.
But word spread and the skin was given away by her husband

to another he couldn't refuse. She raved. The skin returned
via a marauding servant who called her 'mother'. It had changed in colour,
was maybe a donkey, or something worse, and would not rise again.

Decades later grandfather called out in someone's dream to get rid of it—
an agitated soul without rest. When he died his daughters were warned
    against
clothing their father in anything they had bought, lest he be kept
from heaven. *Get it out of the house!* He cried.
Grandmother could not remember the skin.

§

G0P0   (nullipara)

Why have you come here now   with your light, unwieldy throat?

Even though I know your skin is the terrible sound of evening
        its terrible music   cutting from a kitchen window
    where knives slip through hot water like eaves of sea water
glowering between angles of dusk

    there is no measure by which I can take your hand
push out of this nightfall through a garden gate that turns on a spit.

§

Tragedy needs no master—it is the grandmother of invention.
    Vanity   slight as a girl's wrist
weaves it from cruelty   is hewn from a single slight
    so minor that it bears forth its epic image in stone
        from which there is no god or woman to flatter it to sleep.

Umschalter

The child, profligate, rotates her idols.   Sun-facing between sand and sky—
Stone totems, envious moons
    she moistens their eyes with her tongue.

Unmarriageable nests cartwheel   through an ice-age seabed
    over constabularies of sting-tailed reds
                  a remorseless desert.

The sine wave of a snake   predicates.
   What does not heal is inherited   deposited in unlooked-for wells.

   Lone ritualist   of an emptied race,
Her hands cup themselves in prayer
   orative   needing no hour but this.

Amanuensis at the Chromatic Gate

The sea and sky that aspire   unseasonably   to an unaccountable hue
        of solid reasoning, averse to the long-winded nostalgia
and metaphysics of mother-in-laws, cloaked in wind
                                attenuated by a previous century, rise
ascendant in a spine of Bayer blue.

Footed like its master in steel   the exile's preference
        —an imagined elsewhere—flutes its plumes in ochre
and blushes with notable reticence. Delayed here
     the refugee   12.5 tons of leaden metal
               slowly tallies its accounts
as the locals declare it an eyesore.

Integrate? With this face?

The Gate hangs clean against the undeciduous shore.
The earth refuses to modernize.
The vision erodes under the hand that built it.

9 781848 612044